THE
MORTAL INSTRUMENTS
City of Bones
THE OFFICIAL ILLUSTRATED
MOVIE COMPANION

THE
MORTAL INSTRUMENTS
City of Bones

THE OFFICIAL ILLUSTRATED
MOVIE COMPANION

MIMI O'CONNOR

MARGARET K. MCELDERRY BOOKS
NEW YORK   LONDON   TORONTO   SYDNEY   NEW DELHI

MARGARET K. McELDERRY BOOKS

An imprint of Simon & Schuster Children's Publishing Division

1230 Avenue of the Americas, New York, New York 10020

All rights reserved, including the right of reproduction in whole or in part in any form.

Margaret K. McElderry Books is a trademark of Simon & Schuster, Inc.

For information about special discounts for bulk purchases,

please contact Simon & Schuster Special Sales at 1-866-506-1949

or business@simonandschuster.com.

The Simon & Schuster Speakers Bureau can bring authors

to your live event. For more information or to book an event,

contact the Simon & Schuster Speakers Bureau at 1-866-248-3049

or visit our website at www.simonspeakers.com.

Book design by Mike Rosamilia

The text for this book is set in Adobe Caslon Pro.

Manufactured in the United States of America

2 4 6 8 10 9 7 5 3 1

Library of Congress Control Number 2013938856

ISBN 978-1-4424-9398-8 (pbk)

ISBN 978-1-4424-9590-6 (eBook)

CONTENTS

ONE

THE HISTORY OF CITY OF BONES

SITTING ON THE SET OF *THE MORTAL INSTRUMENTS: CITY OF BONES*, THE SERIES'S AUTHOR CASSANDRA CLARE IS QUICK TO ACKNOWLEDGE THE SURREAL NATURE OF THE SCENE SURROUNDING HER. "MOST BOOKS ARE NEVER MADE INTO MOVIES. IT'S A DREAM YOU HAVE WHEN YOU WRITE A BOOK: 'MAYBE SOMEDAY IT'LL BE A MOVIE.' BUT YOU DON'T THINK IT'LL EVER ACTUALLY HAPPEN."

This, from the person whose imagination spawned an entire race of people who are born with angelic blood; an alternate world bubbling just beneath reality and populated by warring factions; a dizzying cast of characters with complicated, overlapping histories; and a labyrinthine plotline so intricate, it has sustained six novels, a new series called The Infernal Devices, and countless other literary spin-offs like the Bane Chronicles, an innovative eBook short story collection in ten parts. Still, she probably couldn't have dreamed up the story that landed her in Toronto, Canada, with major movie stars like Lily Collins, Jamie Campbell Bower, and Jonathan Rhys Meyers (and many more) walking around, sporting Shadowhunter runes on their skin.

Perhaps fittingly, the origins of the epic Shadowhunter chronicle can be found in a

Author of *The Mortal Instruments: City of Bones*, Cassandra Clare

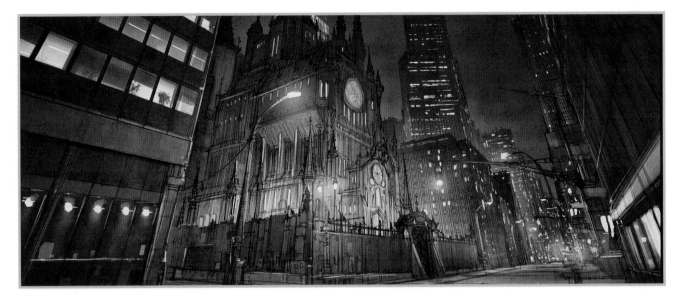

Concept art of the New York Institute by artist Nikolai Lockertsen.

little corner of heroine Clary Fray's big home, New York City. A 2003 visit to a tattoo-artist friend's former workplace in the West Village proved to be highly inspirational for Clare. "She had done this series of very beautiful tattoos based on runes. . . . And she was explaining to me the meaning of each of them and how warriors had once worn them into battle because they believed that the runes would protect them. They would protect them against injury; they would allow them to win out against evil," the writer recalls. "And I thought, 'What if there was a race of people for whom these tattoos really worked? What do they fight? They fight demons, and they use magic. They're this secret group, and they keep the world safe.'"

An unusual custom at the tattoo parlor also helped provide a creative spark, filling Clare's head with images of powerful and magical warriors. "They had a tradition there of having the staff step in paint and track their footprints across the ceiling," she told Blogcritics. "It looked to me like some supernatural battle had taken place with people running across the walls and ceiling. I started working from there on a book that centered on tattoo-based magic."

A longtime fan of the fantasy category, Clare exclusively read the genre as a child, with favorites including Susan Cooper's Dark Is Rising series, C. S. Lewis's Chronicles of Narnia, J. R. R. Tolkien's Lord of the Rings, and Lloyd Alexander's Prydain Chronicles. By the time she walked into that tattoo shop, Clare was no stranger to writing, either: she was then making her living as a freelance journalist, working for publications such as the *Hollywood Reporter*. "I would write light entertainment nonfiction pieces during the day, then come home and work on my fantasy fiction," she told WriteWords. But surprisingly, she didn't have that much experience writing fiction; her previous work included what she describes as a "pretty terrible" romance penned when she was fifteen years old and a single published short story entitled "The Girl's Guide to Defeating the Dark Lord."

Regardless, Clare had a story to tell. "I wanted to write an epic coming-of-age story but with a girl, a heroine, at its center instead of a boy, which is the usual thing. And I wanted to set it in New York City, where I had just moved, because I thought that New York was a city with a beautiful and amazing history," she says. "I wanted to tell a story about characters at that crucial life stage just between adolescence and adulthood, where every choice seems possible. I knew it had to be a coming-of-age story. That's just how I envisioned it," she told Blogcritics. She didn't, however, consciously set out to write a young adult novel. "I just set out to write books," she says. "I found out after I wrote them that they were YA."

FROM THE GET-GO, PUBLISHERS KNEW THIS BOOK WAS SOMETHING SPECIAL.

One year and countless revisions later, Clare had produced ten chapters of what would be her debut novel. It was enough to gain the attention of an agent, who (in a not uncommon move) helped the author further revise the chapters in preparation for submitting the work to publishing houses.

In 2005, sixty pages and a synopsis of *The Mortal Instruments: City of Bones* landed on the desk of editors in New York City and across the world. From the get-go, publishers knew this book was something special. Not only did the international offers for the books start rolling in, Clare began meeting with interested editors from New York's biggest publishing houses, including Margaret K. McElderry Books editor Karen Wojtyla. It didn't take long for the editor to arrive at a decision about the material. "*City of Bones* grabbed me from the start. I think I was about five pages in when I knew I wanted to publish it. It was so smart; the characters' voices were so spot-on. And funny. All that with tremendous action," she says. Pitched as an exotic urban fantasy filled with memorable characters and a love triangle with a twist, Wojtyla felt the novel had tremendous potential to connect with young adult readers. "I think they can see themselves and their friends as these characters, or see themselves as knowing these characters in a more fun and furious version of this world," she says. "And the books are solidly set in this world. It's very real—the books seem to peel back a layer of haze and you see the real world underneath. The characters are so rounded, so well drawn—you really get to care about them. And they are funny and whip smart." Based on the strength of the sample chapters and outline, Wojtyla contracted Clare to write not just one book, but a trilogy. (With bestselling-author status and optioned movie rights not quite yet on the horizon, Clare paid her rent—and got to work.)

Meanwhile, a perfect storm was brewing in the bookselling and book-buying communities. The blockbuster success of titles like J. K. Rowling's Harry Potter series and Stephenie Meyer's Twilight trilogy undeniably proved that both booksellers and readers possessed a virtually insatiable appetite for fantasy, romance, and titles traditionally categorized as young adult novels—so long as they featured compelling characters and excellently crafted story lines. "I think Harry Potter started to tip the scale, but *Twilight* tipped it all the way over," Clare told *Metro*. "*Twilight* has an adult-friendly cover. . . . It knocked down the barriers between the young adult section and the rest of the store."

When the first book in the trilogy, *City of Bones*, released in 2007, it didn't take long before it hit the prestigious *New York Times* bestseller list, where it debuted at number eight. Wojtyla credits three aspects of the book's immediate,

impactful success: Clare's huge online presence and her connection and attention to her fans; the provocative, sexy cover, featuring a bare-chested Shadowhunter; and, of course, a remarkably well-written and engaging story.

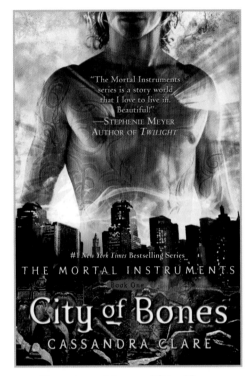

The controversial cover of City of Bones.

The cover of *City of Bones* warrants some attention—there was at least one bookseller who felt that the cover would limit the readership. But in the end, the cover stayed. Bloggers posted the gorgeous image over and over, and the momentum kept building. Eventually, word of this successful coming-of-age fantasy romance reached the offices of Hollywood film executives. "Since the success of the Twilight movies, every producer and every production company has been trying to find their equivalent. So anything that has 'young

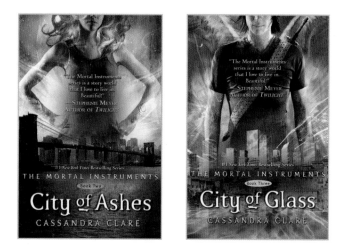

The next four books of the Mortal Instruments series.

adult' in the [description] has been read to death," says *The Mortal Instruments: City of Bones* producer Robert Kulzer.

It took very little convincing to get producer Don Carmody to sign on, particularly because he didn't have to look farther than his own living room to get a sense of both the size and enthusiasm of the book's fan base. "Robert Kulzer mentioned the books to me, and I started checking around and my then-teenage daughters were huge fans," he says. "[They] had grown a bit blasé about the movies I was making, but all of a sudden they were very interested again. The Mortal Instruments—that was what they really, really wanted to see. When I realized they were that audience, I realized how big the audience was for these young adult novels."

In January 2012, the producers developed a newly revised version of the script and scheduled production to begin eight months later in Toronto, Canada.

"I THINK *CITY OF BONES* RESONATES WITH THE YOUNG ADULT AGE GROUP BECAUSE IT'S ABOUT A YOUNG WOMAN FINDING HERSELF AND DISCOVERING WHO SHE REALLY IS. AND ASIDE FROM THE FANTASY ELEMENTS, IT'S SOMETHING THAT IS ATTRACTIVE TO YOUNG ADULTS, WHO ARE ALL LOOKING TO DETERMINE WHO THEY ARE AND WHERE THEY BELONG IN THE GREATER SCHEME OF THINGS."
—PRODUCER DON CARMODY

Finding the right director for the project would be both crucial and challenging. The independent producers needed someone who instinctively understood the project and possessed an impressive track record to help attract interest and financing in the project. Plus, that person had to be able to start immediately. "I was basically looking for [a] genius director who had just come off a big success, who liked the material, and who was ready to look me in the eye and say, 'Let's do this,'" says Kulzer.

And then the fates smiled upon Kulzer again. A high-powered talent agency called the producer and asked if he'd like to meet with Harald Zwart, a director who had recently helmed *The Karate Kid*, a worldwide box office success.

"Sometimes the movie gods just look down on you and make things work. Harald came in with a whole folder of tear sheets and boards that he had put together. He said, 'This is how I see the character of Clary. This is how I see the world. This is my color palette. This is how I would deal with the magic.' It was a two-hour meeting, and after the meeting I walked up to him and said, 'Hey, Harald, I get the sense that you really want to make this movie.' And he said, 'Well, of course. Why do you think I would do all this work and put all this stuff together? I want to make the movie.'

So, in a way, we kind of made the decision right there. This would be his next film. He would drop everything else he was doing and focus on casting and prepping this film for us."

While Zwart is now an expert in all things Nephilim, he started out completely ignorant of The Mortal Instruments phenomenon. "I only heard the sales numbers prior to doing this movie, and being a natural skeptic, I wanted to see for myself," he recalls. "So I just walked into random bookstores, and I saw shelf after shelf [of books]. In certain bookstores they didn't have enough shelf space, so they stacked piles on the floor."

"I SAW SHELF AFTER SHELF [OF BOOKS]. IN CERTAIN BOOKSTORES THEY DIDN'T HAVE ENOUGH SHELF SPACE, SO THEY STACKED PILES ON THE FLOOR." —DIRECTOR HARALD ZWART

Zwart, whose other projects include *One Night at McCool's*, *Agent Cody Banks*, *The Karate Kid*, and several European successes, came to the project with experience and vision. "On the surface, the ideal director for this

Sheehan and Zwart discuss the details of the infirmary scene.

City of Bones: The Official Illustrated Movie Companion

movie . . . should be one of those visual artists. Someone who can create a world. Someone who knows how to deal with special effects. Someone who's done monster movies," says Kulzer. Zwart's unique visual style—as shown in his feature films and special effects from commercial shoots—had Kulzer convinced. But Zwart's enthusiasm also made the director an obvious choice. "What Harald Zwart brought to the table in spades [was] that he was falling in love with the characters. He said, 'I like this world. I want to make what's already written on the page into a film. I don't have to design another world. I don't have to design more creatures. I have my hands full with just what's on the page.' He fell in love with the humanity of the characters and the emotional through-lines that they had."

> **"[ZWART] FELL IN LOVE WITH THE HUMANITY OF THE CHARACTERS AND THE EMOTIONAL THROUGH-LINES THAT THEY HAD."**
> **—PRODUCER ROBERT KULZER**

Writer Clare feels Zwart's interest in and understanding of the complex characters she's drawn make him a superb choice to helm the film adaptation of her novel. "He's incredibly attuned to the emotional lives of the characters, which is something that people forget about a lot in fantasy. They tend to concentrate a lot on the visuals of fantasy, which are fascinating, and he's definitely interested in that. But you can't really substitute visuals—no matter how cool they are—for characters who have rich emotional lives and important relationships with each other. And so I think that Harald is a great director for the project in the sense that what

One of Zwart's early sketches of a Silent Brother

he is extremely interested in is relationships between everyone," she says. "I think it's this interrelationship of all the characters—when you're intrigued by every kind of relationship: the familial, the friend, the romantic relationships—that really makes fantasy feel real."

According to Clare, Zwart was an extremely enthusiastic Mortal Instruments student from the get-go. "The first time I met him in Los Angeles . . . he just immediately launched into

Zwart frames the alley scene with Collins.

A preliminary rendering of the Mortal Instruments logo, by Zwart

all these questions. . . . He was really fascinated to hear about fantasy, how it works, how it has its own rules, how the system of your magic has rules that you have to adhere to once you estab-lish them. . . . It was a lot of fun; we were there talking for, like, six or seven hours. We closed out the restaurant," she recalls. "It's really great to be able to talk to somebody about something that I've thought about almost exclusively for seven or eight years now. This magic system, this world, how it works—it's very real to me. And so to be able to talk to somebody else whose job it is to also make it real is really rewarding."

Zwart and everyone else involved with the production know that making it real and successfully translating Clare's vision to the big screen isn't a job for the fainthearted.

"To me, the key is keeping the characters as real and smart and funny as they are in the books," says Clare's editor, Wojtyla. "And keeping everything grounded in this world, even as your eyes open to this other, fantasy world."

"When you read the novels that Cassandra Clare wrote, there is a sense of just falling into this world of The Mortal Instruments and these Shadowhunters. You spend hours reading page after page, and it's very absorbing," says Kulzer. "There are all these surprises that you encounter on this journey: where these characters come from, where they're going to, how they're all connected. We want to create a similar sense of wonder when you see this movie. I hope people want to stay in that space . . . and go on this incredible journey of discovery."

Back on the *City of Bones* set in Toronto, Clare marvels at the incredible journey she herself has taken and how real, in fact, it all seems. "Writing is a very solitary process,

especially in the beginning. You imagine this world inside your head. You imagine these characters. They come to life inside your head—they become people; they talk—and you feel a little bit as if you're chronicling a story that already exists," she says. "To come

> "YOU SPEND HOURS READING PAGE AFTER PAGE, AND IT'S VERY ABSORBING. THERE ARE ALL THESE SURPRISES THAT YOU ENCOUNTER ON THIS JOURNEY: WHERE THESE CHARACTERS COME FROM, WHERE THEY'RE GOING TO, HOW THEY'RE ALL CONNECTED."
> —PRODUCER ROBERT KULZER

to the set of a movie and to see it in three dimensions instead of the two dimensions that you see in your head—to see the City of Bones and to see these actors, who are walking around dressed as the characters with the runes on their bodies, in character, thinking like the characters—is such an incredible experience. It makes you feel as if you've had a dream, and now you've traveled into that dream and it's become real."

TWO

THE CAST OF CITY OF BONES

TO SAY THAT THE DENIZENS OF CASSANDRA CLARE'S FICTIONAL WORLD ARE A DIVERSE GROUP IS BEYOND UNDERSTATEMENT. VAMPIRES. WEREWOLVES. A HARD-PARTYING BISEXUAL BROOKLYN WARLOCK.

And don't forget the slightly off West Indian witch who lives downstairs, the mentor, the wise-cracking-but-good-hearted "mundie," a couple of badass demon hunters (one male, one female), and a maniacally brilliant and charismatic fallen Shadowhunter. But wait, there's more—a devastatingly attractive, arrogant, gifted, and conflicted young warrior, and finally, the person around whom this entire cast of characters orbits: a striking, yet unassuming, New York City teenager on a breakneck, often harrowing journey of self-discovery and love, who's unaware of her own formidable power and destiny. (And that's not even everyone.)

Finding a cast to inhabit—and do justice to—this dynamic dramatis personae was no

Alec Lightwood (played by Kevin Zegers) confronts Clary inside the Institute.

City of Bones: The Official Illustrated Movie Companion

The hard-partying warlock
Magnus Bane (played by Godfrey
Gao) in his swanky loft apartment

easy task, and not just because of the compelling nature of the characters. "Cassandra Clare created this universe within the world of The Mortal Instruments, and there's a very complex cast of characters. It's almost like an epic spy thriller, for lack of a better analogy, because a lot of these characters get introduced one way, and then you find out that they are someone completely different," explains producer Robert Kulzer.

The intricate nature of the narrative ultimately means that there are no minor characters—in the book or film. "The challenge in casting this film is twofold. There's a very strong central character: Clary Fray leads you through the movie. And then there [are] characters that will only be in the book for one chapter and then you don't see [them] again until book two or book three. But they need to do a good job in [the movie], allowing us to find out what is important for the story to continue. So you need to cast actors that can keep the fans happy, because they all have very strong preconceptions of what these characters look like," explains Kulzer. However, meeting fans' expectations is only part of it; the scene has to deliver dramatically as well. "They have to nail it," says Kulzer. "There's one pivotal scene where one gigantic twist gets arranged—the actor who you cast with this role has to be terrific. . . . So that was part

From left to right: Kulzer, Zwart, and Collins on set, discussing the filming of a scene inside the Institute

of the challenge: that we have a good dozen phenomenal actors in the movie, where they have to nail their scenes and their characters, because otherwise you will have a big hole in the narrative."

But as the saying goes, a journey of a thousand miles begins with a single step. And that first step was finding the perfect actress to play the saga's fiery heroine, Clary Fray.

City of Bones: The Official Illustrated Movie Companion

"Seeing Lily Collins as Clary Fray—for me, we got it one hundred and ten percent right," says Kulzer. The involvement of Collins, a young actress who initially caught the eye of producers with her performances in the films *Priest* and *Abduction*, could be chalked up to a little bit of luck, patience, and, in no small part, the original engrossing narrative crafted by Cassandra Clare.

"I was a fan of the books before I was cast. I had gotten into them, and once you start reading, you can't stop. That's the beauty of Cassie's writing," says Collins. "I heard they were being made into a movie, and Clint Culpepper at Screen Gems asked me if I was interested in them, and I said, 'I love the books. Of course I am.'"

That was back in 2010, but as often happens

> "I WAS A FAN OF THE BOOKS BEFORE I WAS CAST. I HAD GOTTEN INTO THEM, AND ONCE YOU START READING, YOU CAN'T STOP. THAT'S THE BEAUTY OF CASSIE'S WRITING." —COLLINS

in Hollywood, it would take some time for *City of Bones* to find a studio home and be green-lit for production. The delay ended up working in the producers' favor. In the interim, Collins went off to make the "Snow White" adaptation *Mirror Mirror*.

"[That] was, of course, a total blessing for us, because all of a sudden this girl who had two smaller roles in two movies,

she became the co-lead to Julia Roberts," says Kulzer, "and when we went out to actually find financing for the film, you just had to point to the gigantic billboard on Sunset Boulevard where you saw Lily Collins on one end and Julia Roberts on the other end. Her value increased dramatically with that movie."

girl, but she's got such incredible talent that she makes that character believable," offers producer Don Carmody. "She's not winking at it; she's not going overboard; she's not trying to play a superhero. She's just an American girl that finds herself in this incredible circumstance and goes for it, because she has no other choice. . . . And

Producer Don Carmody and Collins inside the club Pandemonium.

When Clare learned the news of Collins's casting, she felt the selection was spot-on. "I was delighted, because I thought she just jumped out at me as looking exactly like Clary did in my head," the writer says.

"Lily Collins—she's the all-American

she's not unafraid, but she's not cowering, either. So she's a great heroine."

The heavy responsibility of playing a character that millions of fans adore (and have already envisioned for themselves) is not lost on the actress. Collins takes some comfort in the fact that she herself was a Mortal Instruments devotee before a single page of the screenplay existed. "It's great to have been a fan of the series first. It's having a fan be cast as a heroine [people] admire so much," she says. "I feel like I've lived with Clary for longer than just being a character of a movie that I'm playing. It's really a girl that I've gotten to know through the books for a while."

Once the decision of who would play the movie's female protagonist was settled, an even more daunting casting decision loomed: who would bring to life her irrepressible, devastatingly attractive, otherworldly guide to the Shadow World? Finding an actor who could portray the many moods (and smokin' hotness) of Jace Wayland would be no easy task.

"It was one of the tougher casting decisions we had to make, because he's written as an incredibly handsome but incredibly intelligent young man. And that's the key. He is a young man. But he's wise beyond his years because of all the Shadowhunter history," explains Carmody. "And at the same time, he has a certain sardonic point of view. . . . It's a very refreshing take. He's noble but not that noble."

Fortunately, Collins, armed with both her deep knowledge of Jace from reading the series as well as the inside track on who was coming up in young Hollywood, jumped at the chance to assist in the search for the proper Jace. "She was really interested and engaged in trying to help us find Jace. She said, 'I want to know when I'm in the room with this guy that we have that chemistry.' So she almost became our casting associate," says Kulzer.

One actor mentioned early in the search was Jamie Campbell Bower, who had recently performed in the Twilight series and possessed what Kulzer thought of as "an otherworldly quality." Like many, he read for the part. "And then we actually did . . . what's called a chemistry read with Lily Collins," recalls Kulzer. "And it's no exaggeration: sparks were flying. There was an intensity; there was a kind of arrogance that only someone who has experienced what it means to be the best-looking guy in a room [has]. How automatically every man's and every woman's

> "I FEEL LIKE I'VE LIVED WITH CLARY FOR LONGER THAN JUST BEING A CHARACTER OF A MOVIE THAT I'M PLAYING. IT'S REALLY A GIRL THAT I'VE GOTTEN TO KNOW THROUGH THE BOOKS FOR A WHILE."
> —COLLINS

Campbell Bower poses as the fierce, hooded, and weaponed-out Jace Wayland.

eyes are drawn to you. You have to have experienced that to really play that. And Jamie has that in spades."

In addition to that considerable confidence and charm, Bower also brought a unique take on the role of Jace. "Jamie Campbell Bower had a different idea of how he would interpret Jace. He wanted him to have this elegance—this almost balletic [quality], a dancer's elasticity and fluidity in his movements," says Kulzer.

The young actor, cast a year and three months ahead of shooting, immediately got to work developing his character—both mentally and physically—and putting his own stamp on the young Shadowhunter.

From left to right: Isabelle Lightwood (played by Jemima West), Alec, and Jace, hunting a demon inside Pandemonium

"My interpretation of Jace is, he's a young boy; he's a rock star, almost. And I didn't want him to be the archetypal, butch, somewhat-out-of-shape-but-somewhat-in-shape kind of jock that we see in a lot of movies. I wanted him to be lean, I wanted every single part of him that you saw to be one hundred percent muscle—no fat, no nothing, just lean and fast. He's wily and he's crazy and he

has this bizarre look in his eyes," the actor explains. "I wanted that to be represented in the way that he [looked], so I trained super-hard. . . . It was a lot of physical effort for me, and it was hard. It's hard-core to do that to your body, but it paid off. . . . I'm really happy with the results."

Of course, Bower knows that his embodiment of Jace will be measured against the many millions of Jaces conjured in the imaginations of *City of Bones* readers. "With any job that you step into, there should always be a level of apprehension or fear. That . . . is only heightened when you step into a role that already has a fan base behind it," the actor admits. "But I think you have to remember at the end of the day that you're not going to be everyone's personal choice. You're just not. What you have to do is go in there and do the hardest possible work that you can do in order to bring that character to life."

Every great story has a great villain, and *City of Bones* really brings it when it comes to the baddies. Leading the charge, of course, is the Shadowhunter extraordinaire who turned more than a bit twisted, Valentine Morgenstern. But unlike most evildoers on page and screen (think Harry Potter's Voldemort or *Star Wars*'s Darth Vader), Valentine is seductive in every sense of the word.

"He's not some drooling, evil character or just some incredibly wicked mega-villain. His danger lies in his charm," explains Carmody. "He represents everything the Shadowhunters should not be. But yet he has

Valentine Morgenstern (played by Jonathan Rhys Meyers) inside the Institute library

managed to get all of these people to follow him and to go down that path of darkness rather than light. His danger lurks in that he's able to convince people to do what they should not be doing."

"We wanted someone who was terribly handsome, who has that sort of presence and edge. There's a pretty short list—there's maybe a handful of actors out there who have that," says Kulzer of the search for the perfect actor to play the movie's villain. "So we were going through a list and thinking, 'Who has that? Who has this kind of charisma that when you speak to women and you mention the name of an actor they go, 'Oooh, I like him.'"

Author Cassandra Clare on set with a runed-out Meyers

City of Bones: The Official Illustrated Movie Companion

The name Jonathan Rhys Meyers surfaced quickly. "[Women] all 'Oooh' because there's a sort of sense of danger." Sex appeal and natural charisma aside, Meyers also brought serious acting credentials to the weighty role, experience with action sequences from his work on the Showtime series *The Tudors*, and even a facility with sword fighting.

A fan of Meyers's work going back to the 1998 film *Velvet Goldmine*, Clare was thrilled to learn the Irish actor had been cast as Valentine. "He is fantastic at evoking a sort of evil reasonableness. So that even though you know that what he's saying is fundamentally, morally wrong on some level, you want to agree with him because he has this intense charisma," she says. "I felt that that was something that Valentine really needed to have. You had to understand why all these theoretically good people had followed him and been part of his circle." And, the author reports, Meyers easily passed the "Oooh" test with fans. "I have to admit, when I first posted online, 'Jonathan Rhys Meyers is going to be our Valentine,' a lot of people wrote back to me and said, 'Well, I would join the circle if he was running it.' So I feel like he's a good poster boy for his cause."

Every story of magic set in the real world has at least one character who steps back to ask, "Wait a minute. What on earth is going on here!?" They stand in for the audience, pointing out the complete insanity that surrounds them. In *City of Bones*, that person is the lovable (and lovesick) Simon Lewis, Clary's lifelong best friend with a quick wit and a crush on his buddy. The only true "mundane" pulled into a perilous adventure filled with Shadowhunters, vampires, demons, and many more otherworldly creatures, Simon is a fan favorite.

"[He's] the only normal guy in the whole script," says Robbie Sheehan, the actor selected to bring Simon to life on the big screen. "He [has] the only sense of perspective against this entire magical world. . . . And there's a lot of fun in playing that."

"Simon has an almost Superman–Clark Kent duality because he is the kind of geeky guy with the glasses who has the funny line.

> THE ONLY TRUE "MUNDANE" PULLED INTO A PERILOUS ADVENTURE FILLED WITH SHADOWHUNTERS, VAMPIRES, DEMONS, AND MANY MORE OTHERWORLDLY CREATURES, SIMON IS A FAN FAVORITE.

He's a bit of a stumbler and hasn't quite found his place in the world yet. But he will [later] evolve into this powerful man," says Kulzer, referencing the character's evolution over the course of The Mortal Instruments series. "And so there is this kind of duality in the character. . . . So even if he appears slightly nerdy, you can look behind his glasses [and see] there is the potential of a real man and a real hero."

With Simon the object of so much fan adoration, it seemed natural to ask readers who they thought should play Clary's endearing, bespectacled sidekick. "In the casting process of Simon, we relied heavily on the fans," says Kulzer. "And early on we heard it over

Simon, a mundane, inside the Institute

Clary and Simon in the infirmary as Clary heals from a vicious demon attack

"IN THE CASTING PROCESS OF SIMON, WE RELIED HEAVILY ON THE FANS," SAYS KULZER. "AND EARLY ON WE HEARD IT OVER AND OVER AND OVER AGAIN: 'WHAT ABOUT ROBBIE SHEEHAN?'"—PRODUCER ROBERT KULZER

and over and over again: 'What about Robbie Sheehan?'; 'What about Robbie Sheehan?'; 'We love Robbie Sheehan.'"

A young Irish actor who flew a bit under the radar, Sheehan had garnered attention for his work as Nathan Young on the UK show *Misfits*. A tape of Sheehan surrounded by screaming girls at a movie premiere (courtesy of his agent, of course) plus Clare's own burgeoning enthusiasm about the idea of Sheehan as Simon resulted in the studio flying the actor to Los Angeles for an audition. "We had the luxury of doing a chemistry test with Lily and with Jamie, and they both immediately said, 'Robbie Sheehan is Simon. There's no question,'" says Kulzer. "So it was kind of a socialist casting process."

"Simon has really funny one-liners, and he has a slightly skewed sense of humor," says Kulzer. "And Robbie just does that perfectly. Everything he does, there's a little bit of a joke at the end, a little bit of a smirk. And he just has perfect comedic timing."

Clare agrees, adding, "Robbie is an absolutely terrific Simon. He has that funny energy and that passion and enthusiasm and accessibility that Simon has."

Jace, of course, has some BFFs as well. (As much as Jace can have BFFs, that is.) His posse consists of the brother-sister duo Alec and Isabelle Lightwood, who are at his side battling demons and risking their lives, day in and day out. As with any crime-fighting outfit, the rapport among the players would be crucial.

"The chemistry between Jace and Alec and Isabelle is that of kind-of-siblings that have been growing up together, but instead of fighting over cereal, they fight over who gets to kill this demon or that demon," explains Kulzer. "So they have much bigger stakes. And then there's a kind of comedic banter between the three of them. But also, they need to be very strong physically, and they have to have a certain gravitas."

For the ravishing and tough Isabelle, Jemima West was an early choice. "She has

this great voice and this great presence, and feels like this almost aristocratic person [when] you meet her," says Kulzer. "She did a phenomenal job in her audition, and we cast her pretty much right off the bat."

Finding the right Alec would take a bit longer, although Kevin Zegers, who would eventually land the role, had worked with producer Kulzer on the movie *Wrong Turn* back in 2003 and made an impression on the executive. "It was this gritty survival-horror movie. We had a young cast, and even then the line outside Kevin's trailer was the longest. He had the most fans. So I always sort of kept thinking about him." As the *City of Bones* script was revised to feature characters slightly older than those in the book, the more mature Zegers suddenly became a casting possibility, and he scored the Alec Lightwood role.

"I just delight in watching . . . how they all interact with each other," says Carmody of the Shadowhunting cast members. "They've really become a close unit, and, you know, a look is as significant as a sentence [between them]."

Bower confirms that the bonds are strong between the Shadowhunting crew, both on-screen and off. "We all share qualities of the characters that we're playing. . . . The three Shadowhunters, they get along very well, even though they have these somewhat conflicting

Tough-as-nails brother/sister Shadowhunter combo Alec and Isabelle Lightwood.

Jocelyn Fray (played by Lena Headey) floats in a mysterious sleep.

Jocelyn as a younger Shadowhunter

qualities," says Bower. "And it's the same in life. . . . I do feel very connected to Kevin and Jemima, and we are like a pack. We are very, very protective over each other. And that's a really nice feeling to have. To be watched over."

Casting the part of Clary's mom, Jocelyn Fray, presented its own unique challenge. Namely, fans of The Mortal Instruments series know she's a powerful woman not to be messed with (as described in later installments), but in *City of Bones*, she pretty much just lies there and does nothing.

"A large part of what she does is be unconscious. . . . So it's really [about] finding an actress where you say, 'I'm looking at her, and she's just unconscious . . . but something about this woman tells me that she can kick some serious ass,'" explains Kulzer. Lena Headey, who could do beautiful and incredibly tough, as evidenced by her work as Sarah Connor in the television series *Terminator: The Sarah Connor Chronicles* and the film *300*, would ultimately claim the role of Clary's overprotective mom, who has a big secret. "[Lena] has that. An elegant, modern woman who also happens to be a major action heroine," says Kulzer.

The list of accomplished and notable actors in the *City of Bones* cast goes on. There's Jared Harris, perhaps best known as the tragic Lane Pryce on the hit show *Mad Men*, giving life to Hodge, the senior counselor to the

Above: Hodge Starkweather (played by Jared Harris) inside the Institute

Right: Madame Dorothea (played by CCH Pounder), the elusive prophetess

young Shadowhunters. "I feel like he will capture Hodge's essential dilemma," says Clare. "[Hodge] is extremely conflicted about what he believes the Shadowhunters should be doing . . . and I feel if there's anyone who's really great at capturing shades of gray morally, Jared is that guy." CCH Pounder takes on the role of the mysterious Madame Dorothea with gusto. "Harald from the beginning said,

'If we can get CCH Pounder to play this role, she would be perfect,'" says Kulzer. "There is a kind of gravitas that she brings to the table that we knew she had. What we didn't quite know is how much fun she would have with playing a character that is literally being

Pangborn (left, played by Kevin Durand) and Blackwell (right, played by Robert Maillet), two of Valentine's loyal thugs

taken over by a demon." Providing brawn to Valentine's brains are the terrifying Emil Pangborn and Samuel Blackwell, played by the tall, muscular Kevin Durand and Robert Maillet, respectively. "These are great choices for these characters, because I wouldn't want to tangle with them in a dark alley," says Clare.

After assembling the perfect mix of performers to bring *City of Bones* to life on film, everyone—including the novel's dedicated fans—feels the roster of talent more than does justice to the story and the characters. "Fortunately, most of [the fans] signed on with our casting choices and are very supportive," says Carmody. "I think it helped that we brought Cassandra into the process and made her a part of it. We didn't shove the author out. We embraced her, because nobody knows this story like she does, and she was really great in the casting process in

City of Bones: The Official Illustrated Movie Companion

Director Zwart and Meyers discuss Valentine's emergence from the Portal.

helping us bridge the communication with the fans, because she's been very open and inclusive of them."

Perhaps most pleased, however, is director Zwart, who always maintained that it is the characters and their emotional journey that makes *City of Bones* such a riveting story.

"What was really important for me was to have really great actors," he concludes. "It's a movie where you can get carried away in the special effects and the fantasy of it, but unless the actors are just superb, it—it wouldn't work for me, at least. So I'm very happy to have really great actors inhabiting all the roles."

THREE

THE PLACES AND PROPS OF *CITY OF BONES*

PART OF WHAT MAKES THE UNIVERSE OF *CITY OF BONES* SO ENTHRALLING IS THAT IT IS LIMITED ONLY BY CASSANDRA CLARE'S CONSIDERABLE IMAGINATION. IN OTHER WORDS, IT'S NOT LIMITED AT ALL: A SPIRE CAN SEEM TO EXTEND ALMOST INFINITELY; A WARRIOR CAN WIELD A CRYSTAL SWORD WITH EASE; A SPRAWLING, BEAUTIFULLY APPOINTED GOTHIC CATHEDRAL CAN SIT IN THE MIDDLE OF THE CITY (AT LEAST, FOR THOSE WHO CAN ACTUALLY SEE BEYOND THE GLAMOUR THAT CONCEALS IT).

The namesake of the book and movie: the City of Bones

Set and prop designers, however, are not so lucky. These film professionals are bound by real-world constraints, such as the laws of physics, shooting schedules, and budgets.

"One of the mandates that we had was to be as true to the books as possible," says the film's prop master, James Murray. "We can never translate what's on the page to the screen exactly the way it is in the book, but we want to get as close to it as possible."

When tackling the important job of designing the assortment of weapons to be featured in the film, Murray first looked to the novel's community of fans for inspiration. "Part of the process of that was doing a lot of research about what the fans were thinking the stuff looked like. The different props, like the steles and the blades. Listening to their input on the Web . . . and reading different ideas and directions that they thought it was going to go."

Creating weapons that looked good, met with fans' expectations, and adhered to the logic of the movie's universe was crucial to the filmmakers. It also took up a tremendous amount of time. "The amount of sword meetings that we had on this movie: What is the blade that can kill a demon? What is the blade that can kill a vampire? What is the blade that can kill a werewolf? It goes on and on," says producer Robert Kulzer. "I mean,

the amount of blade discussions that we had would blow your mind."

After reading the script, it was clear to Murray which prop would be most difficult to craft. "I was flipping through the script, and I kept reading [about] these glass swords. Everywhere there was a glass sword," he recalls. "It's not like you can go to the sword store and buy a glass sword. We had to design it specifically for our needs." And they had to do it in seven weeks.

> "THE AMOUNT OF SWORD MEETINGS THAT WE HAD ON THIS MOVIE: WHAT IS THE BLADE THAT CAN KILL A DEMON? WHAT IS THE BLADE THAT CAN KILL A VAMPIRE? WHAT IS THE BLADE THAT CAN KILL A WEREWOLF? IT GOES ON AND ON. I MEAN, THE AMOUNT OF BLADE DISCUSSIONS THAT WE HAD WOULD BLOW YOUR MIND."
> —PRODUCER ROBERT KULZER

Using a design approved by director Harald Zwart and production designer

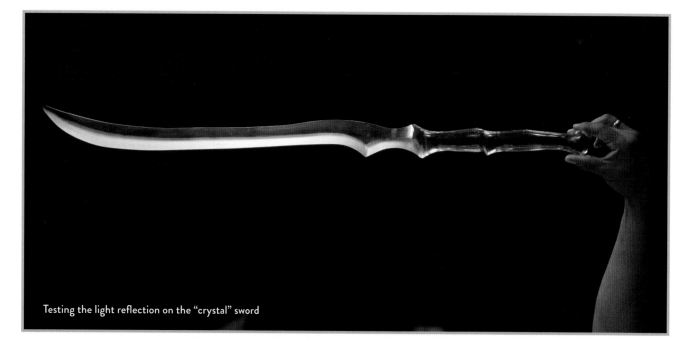

Testing the light reflection on the "crystal" sword

François Séguin, the props department created a wooden model of the weapon; from that, plastic test swords were molded to assess the prop's overall look and grip. An ill-fated early foray into making a glass sword for a few special shots revealed that using real glass for all the swords was never really an option. "We opted for acrylic over glass because glass was too hard to mold with and too heavy. The large sword would have weighed seventeen pounds and the actors wouldn't have been able to use it on set. And it probably would have snapped in many places," explains Murray.

Three hours of polishing with a rubbing compound gave each acrylic sword the crystal-clear appearance of glass; the final product ultimately proved to be a little too convincing. "The first day of shooting, we brought the blades to set, and they were too clear," says Murray. "We ended up taking them back to the shop and then buffing out the blade to give the blade a bit of texture, so that it just would catch the light differently."

In the end, the props department created sixty swords, including long weapons to be held with two hands, short daggers, and swords of different lengths to be used for the CGI sequences. "Anytime we had any fight sequences when someone was fighting a demon, we had to cut the blades down to allow for the computer graphics team to draw in the blade," explains Murray. "So depending on what the action was, we could pull out a different dagger, or different sword length on how far in the stab was. We did three versions to cover ourselves on set, so we weren't cutting down swords. Because we didn't want to build all these expensive

City of Bones: The Official Illustrated Movie Companion

acrylic glass-looking swords and have to cut them down on the day."

No respectable Shadowhunter goes anywhere without a stele, either. "We needed to stay away from anything that looked like a wand . . . and any other kind of wizardy thing," says Murray of the stele design process. For that reason, crafting the instrument out of wood was out of the question. Murray selected metal—specifically poured pewter, in the case of Jace's stele—as the tool's material and added a crystal at the tip. "We wanted to do some-thing crystalline at the end because there's a bunch of scenes where it lights up," says Murray. "We felt that if it was just a whole pewter bar it would look weird lighting up from the end, almost like a laser pointer." Finally, the addition of rune decorations gave the stele a handcrafted and aged look, while a programmable control box connected to bright LED lights enabled the tool to light up, dim, and flicker as needed—but not without heating up fairly quickly. "Superbright LEDs get really hot . . . so we're limited to the amount of time

Jace brandishes the "crystal" sword inside Pandemonium.

Isabelle destroys ravens that are invading through the Institute dome.

we can shoot with [the stele]," says Murray. "You can't have it on for more than five minutes without the stele actually getting warm in [Jamie's] hand."

Yet another tool in the Shadowhunter arsenal is the witchlight: part handy flashlight, part demon repellent. To create the prop, Murray went the geological route. "We ended up going out and buying a bunch of crystals and rocks and showing them to the director," he explains. Zwart selected a favorite, which was then cast in resin and given a crystallized appearance. An inexpensive LED light similar to those found in bike lights provided a low-tech but convincing source of illumination rugged enough to withstand the drops and throws dictated by the script. "It was a twelve-dollar little LED drilled into a witchlight and it actually worked. It was one of those last-minute things that at the end of the day totally paid off," says Murray.

Sometimes the filmmaking process

Jace's witchlight provdes a way to see inside the dark Hotel Dumort.

City of Bones: The Official Illustrated Movie Companion

requires producing multiple versions of the same prop. On the *City of Bones* set, that prop was Jocelyn's tarot cards, one of which bears significance in the story. Playing such a pivotal role in the film, the cards get a lot of screen time, and the action surrounding them necessitated making cards in varying sizes and conditions.

The props department produced one standard deck for use early in the film, as well as several cards with strategically placed blood splatter patterns for the movie's later scenes. "The blood is not random. It's been painted on exactly so we can see a bit of the card," says Murray. Action scenes called for oversize cards (which are easier to see when filmed), and the sequence of Clary pulling an item from a card required that one be created specifically for that action—achieved with an in-camera optical illusion, not special effects—as well as a post-pull card, one missing the image of the cup. With artwork that was originally drawn by Leo Leibelman, each one of the cards was hand-painted by the art department.

If *City of Bones* has a star prop, it's without question the Mortal Cup—after all, the quest for it drives the action of the entire movie. A sacred relic of the Shadowhunters, it's been around for thousands of years, and it had to look like it. "The mandate for the Mortal Cup was

to keep it looking as organic as possible. So it didn't look like it was machined," says Murray. "The glass would be hand blown; everything would be more or less old-school in its artistry."

With that goal in mind, the production enlisted artisans to custom-make the central prop. The entire process of crafting the cup took six weeks, beginning with the approval of a wooden model made to assess the size and grip. A glassblower then produced the cup portion, while a jeweler cast the remainder of the prop in bronze and then applied silver and gold plating to it. Several versions of the cup were made, with one "hero" cup reserved for close-ups, and still others for use during the action sequences. "Because there was so much action on the cup, we had to get stunt cups made as well because this cup was going everywhere," explains Murray. "We poured quick, plastic versions that we could throw around and use for all the stunt action. There was no way we could use [the hero] cup because it would just get damaged."

As the person charged with creating the fantastic and urban settings of *City of Bones* (as imagined by production designer François Séguin), art director Anthony Ianni never thought his job was going to be easy; he just didn't know it would be so intense. "This is a very, very ambitious project," he says. "As soon as I started working on it, I

Clary and Simon walking in "Brooklyn,"
but really on a street in Toronto

realized right away that this was going to be something a little bit bigger. It's not only the number of sets and the size of the sets that we've constructed, but François's vision is very, very heavily detailed."

Which is why all the sets—ranging from a vampire lair or a cathedral-turned-demon-killer-headquarters to a packed soothsayer's apartment, a subterranean graveyard, and an incredibly romantic greenhouse—possess an undeniable sumptuous and richly textured quality.

The producers of *City of Bones* found many of the film's locations in and around Toronto, Canada, where the movie was filmed. A particularly lucky find was the set for the Hotel Dumort, once a high-end hotel named the Royal Connaught. "It's actually an

"THIS IS A VERY, VERY AMBITIOUS PROJECT, AS SOON AS I STARTED WORKING ON IT. I REALIZED RIGHT AWAY THAT THIS WAS GOING TO BE SOMETHING A LITTLE BIT BIGGER. IT'S NOT ONLY THE NUMBER OF SETS AND THE SIZE OF THE SETS THAT WE'VE CONSTRUCTED, BUT FRANÇOIS'S VISION IS VERY, VERY HEAVILY DETAILED."
—ART DIRECTOR ANTHONY IANNI

Concept art of Simon hanging in the Hotel Dumort by artist Nikolai Lockertsen

abandoned hotel. . . . We had to clean it up so that it was fit for us to be in, and then the art department came back in and dirtied it all up again," says producer Don Carmody. "But the basic structure was there. It's a very creepy place, but also, immediately, it's a hotel. And it's like somebody walked away and just let it go to the elements."

"It was a disaster when we first walked in," says Ianni. "The only thing we really had to do was go in there and paint the walls down to that very dirty kind of aged look that we wanted to bring to the vampire world. . . . Once we cleaned the existing cement and dirt out we had to bring in fresh dirt, and dressing for the sets. So it was a very roundabout way of getting the place dirty again."

Creating Java Jones and Pandemonium would prove to be less labor intensive. A Queens Street café in Toronto outfitted with new lounge furniture and a four-by-sixteen-foot sign (to cover the storefront's exist-

The entrance to the Hotel Dumont, with a clever name change

ing one) easily transformed into Clary and Simon's favorite coffee shop, and downtown club Maison Mercer provided the nightclub setting where Clary gets her first glimpse of the Shadowhunters' deadly prowess. "We just went to town in Toronto to find the most Goth, pierced, and tattooed people we could

For the memorable (and extremely romantic) greenhouse scene in which Clary and Jace finally share a kiss, the production found the perfect location: an early twentieth-century greenhouse located in Toronto's Allan Gardens Conservatory. There was just one problem: as the setting for a scene featuring exotic Shadowhunter floral specimens, it didn't really contain any flowers. "It's very green. There's a lot of banana and palm, but essentially very little flower or anything of any color," says Ianni. "So we had our greens department pick up a whole bunch of silk flowers of various colors and shapes, and they spent about two or three days in there

find, and we filled up one of the clubs with them," says Zwart. "It worked really well."

Clary walks around inside the Pandemonium club.

just dressing it around the flowers that existed. We had to hire the actual people that worked there to do the placement of it because we weren't allowed to actually walk onto their gardens."

"I'm sure [the Shadowhunters] have plants and seeds that no one else has, so I wanted slightly other-wordly, *Avatar*-ish plants in there," says Zwart. While some of the more fanciful flowers in the scene are computer-generated, many are real-world creations of the set decorators.

"We picked up a bunch of weird cabbage, romaine lettuce, and some twigs, and we stuck them all together, and it became something completely different than what it started out as," explains Ianni. "It looks beautiful. It's a really wonderful set."

Finding a single location to serve as the Institute, with its wide variety of interiors, would prove impossible. No fewer than three settings made up the Shadowhunter's HQ, with the University of Toronto's Knox College providing the infirmary and interior entrance; portions of the downtown Gothic revival landmark and museum Casa Loma

Clary and Jace look on as the greenhouse blooms.

serving as the relic room, bedrooms, and hallways; and sets constructed at Toronto's Cinespace Film Studios acting as the library, the dome, the dungeon, and the building's exterior.

One of the advantages of building sets in a studio is that you can create anything you want, exactly the way you want it. "We always kept the notion that we needed to be architecturally sound. We couldn't just do creatively weird things," says Ianni, noting director Zwart's commitment to realism. "But we allowed ourselves the freedom to put in the types of details that we wouldn't necessarily find in the real world." The library set, for example, is full of richly embellished pieces, such as the steel door to the Portal (which is actually constructed of

The intricate set of the City of Bones

The Institute library,
with a statue of the angel Raziel

"For the angel Raziel I wanted something very special. Not your average Romanesque statue you find on any street corner in Italy, but something unique and darker. On a random search I came across this incredible artist, Kris Kuksi, and I called him right away. He loved the project and worked months creating our strange and dark and very complex statue of the angel Raziel." —Director Harald Zwart

Styrofoam and wood, painted to look like brass and steel). "It's about a foot and a half thick, and has this incredible amount of detail in terms of the carvings on the surfaces, both inside and out," says Ianni. The "marble" columns on the library set are yet another example of both cinematic deception and Séguin's baroque aesthetic; looming cardboard tubes were used to mimic concrete posts, while sculptural crow elements decorate the base, and paper printed with a marbled pattern transforms the cardboard into a polished stone.

A closer look at the statue of Raziel

Madame Dorothea's apartment, also constructed in the studio, reflects a similar detailed vision, albeit a vastly more cluttered one. The witch's abode is stuffed with occult memorabilia, spiritual icons, antiques, skulls, and more. "The set decorators did a great job. . . . They just packed it, and it looked fantastic when the camera got in there," recalls Ianni, who feels Séguin's selection of dark, saturated wallpaper in gold and greens created the perfect mood for the set.

Bursting at the seams with stuff, Dorothea's apartment is an unfortunate place to have a monumental fight. But that's exactly what happens there, and the crew designed the set with that heavy-duty destruction in mind. "We built multiples on certain things that we know [would be broken]. . . . They choreograph the stunt, and then we say, 'What can we do to provide things that are going to break away and crash? We can build a stunt chair out of balsa wood, or a stool out of balsa wood that won't hurt.' There's all kinds of breakaway glass and dishes and plates that people can crash into that will be completely harmless to the actors," explains Ianni. "It's very well choreographed. We have to know exactly where they're going because if we want to have a breakaway cabinet or something like that, we need to know that they're going to be smashing into this wall,

A peek at some of the oddities held at Madame Dorothea's

The Places and Props of *City of Bones*

The living room set of Madame Dorothea's apartment

Madame Dorothea looks at
a broken door in this scene.

and that's very specific [to] how that has to be made."

Even if a set isn't in a movie for a long time, that doesn't necessarily mean it gets less attention. Case in point: the set for the location that gives the movie its name, the City of Bones. With a design inspired by the Parisian catacombs, the detailed set took two months to build—the longest of any produced for the film. The crew reproduced mausoleums

Madame Dorothea prepares to read Clary's fortune.

from a Hamilton, Ontario, graveyard, and employed multiple painting techniques to give 130 plastic skulls and hundreds of artificial bones a realistic and aged appearance. "Oftentimes it's equated to the value of the set. It's not just the amount of screen time," Ianni says of the set's labor-to-exposure ratio.

"If we can get a big punch on a set, even for two minutes of the movie, it's well worth it. It takes the movie up to a different level, and I think we achieve that with [the City of Bones]."

At the very least, the task of the art director on any film is to create sets that both look amazing on film and effortlessly transport the audience out of the theater and into another place. It's even better when the actors and crew forget they're on a set too. "Whenever there's the opportunity to develop a set that the cast feels is very realistic, it adds to their sense of reality," says Ianni. "So much so that when we start putting in the special effects, like dripping water and smoke and 'moldy' paint, it really brings them to a level beyond what would be [on] a standard set."

When people arrived at the Institute dungeon set (built in the basement of the studio) and were less than thrilled to be working there, Ianni couldn't have been happier. "It feels great. It feels wonderful because it *looked* dirty, but it was clean," he says. "For them to walk in there and say, 'This is going to be horrible, I don't want to work here'—it feels good."

FOUR

THE COSTUMES AND MAKEUP OF *CITY OF BONES*

WHAT DOES A MODERN-DAY VAMPIRE WEAR? HOW ABOUT A DEMON FROM ANOTHER DIMENSION? OR, FOR THAT MATTER, MEMBERS OF A NEWLY CONCEIVED RACE THAT'S HALF-HUMAN, HALF-ANGEL?

These are just some of the questions the costume designer for the film adaptation of *City of Bones* faced. Gersha Phillips, the person who would take on that job, was up for and excited by the challenge. "I really liked the idea that it was a world that we didn't know. . . . It was something that we could totally start from scratch and do what we wanted to do," she explains. "There were no laws or anything written for it, so it was a great opportunity to be very creative. Yes, we've seen many of those characters before in different films, but it was also a chance to do something slightly different with some of them, which was interesting.

Gersha Phillips outfits Kevin Durand.

The young Shadowhunters in their Shadowhunter attire

Especially the Shadowhunters, because they're an unknown entity."

"I had a meeting with [Gersha], and I instantly saw that she was perfect for the job, because she had a really good sense of fashion," recalls director Harald Zwart. "I wanted it to be not only a great-looking movie, but I love the idea of these Shadowhunters as a bit of a fash-ion statement. And I think she did that really well. When you see all these wardrobes, you say, 'Actually, that looks like tomorrow's new jacket or tomorrow's new pair of pants.'... It's a goth look with a really sensible touch."

When designing the costumes for the Shadowhunters, Phillips felt it was essential that the clothes be both original and durable. (After all, this is the wardrobe of an entirely

Phillips works on West's costume.

new race of people from the fictional country of Idris, who happen to spend most of their time battling demons.) "I wanted [the costumes] to look like stuff that we haven't seen before, that we couldn't buy anywhere," she explains. "But also, they had to have this quality because they're warriors. They're born and bred to

> "THEY'RE WARRIORS. THEY'RE BORN AND BRED TO FIGHT, SO EVERYTHING THAT THEY WEAR IS FOR THAT SORT OF ACTIVITY."
> —COSTUME DESIGNER GERSHA PHILLIPS

fight, so everything that they wear is for that sort of activity." (On a practical note, the costumes accommodated the actors' frequently frenetic movements during filming with hidden knit panels, inseams, and padding, which made the garments lighter and facilitated their movement in action scenes.)

For Jamie Campbell Bower, both looking and feeling good in his costume was crucial to delivering his best performance. "I feel more connected to the role of Jace than I've ever felt connected to any other character. So for me, it was important to be able to feel comfortable in what I was wearing whilst also still having an ethereal quality and looking 'badass,'" says the actor. "Stepping into the costume is the beginning

The Vampire Lieutenant (played by Elyas M'Barek) in full getup

Jace shows Clary his witchlight.

of your day. That is what puts you in the head-space; that's what you do when you're alone, so you have to be able to put [your costume] on and automatically feel in that character."

Dressing a vampire with any originality is tough these days. It's been done. A lot. Phillips's solution? Go contemporary. "We did a very fashion[able] take on them," she says. The designer looked to names such as Gucci and Alexander McQueen for ideas on crafting updated metropolitan vampire garb. "We took [McQueen's] frock coat and made it out of leather, which I thought gave it more of an urban feel, as opposed to completely looking like a period piece. [We were] taking period pieces and redoing them in contemporary fabrics and contemporary styles. Just

giving them that edge. . . . We gave every-thing what I call the 'Diesel breakdown.'"

For the Shadowhunters' costumes, Phillips drew inspiration from designers such as Carol Christian Poell, Boris Bidjan Saberi, Gareth Pugh, and Rick Owens, and stumbled upon a fashion movement in the process. "I was in a fabric store in New York . . . and I was looking for very specific types of things that were distressed and just more interesting. The gentleman I was dealing with said, 'You should check out this website called Style-Zeitgeist.' And [I did], and I realized that it was all the same designers I'd been looking at. . . . [StyleZeitgeist] is sort of the new-age-goth look," she says. "It has a goth feel to it, but it has this whole other really avant-garde cut to it that's really cool and interesting, and I found that really inspiring." Metal details on the Shadowhunters' ensembles, such as buckles—acquired from a local Toronto sex shop—and harnesses made from shiny stain-less steel were also distressed to give them an aged, weathered appearance.

Outfitting Lily Collins as Clary Fray required taking her from groovy-but-casual Brooklyn gal to fledgling Shadowhunter. "It was really important that she looked cool and interesting and hip and not too boring," says Phillips of Clary's fashion sense. In an effort to stay true to the book, the designer even dyed the sweater Collins wears in the opening sequence of the film to the color green, Clary's favorite hue. But the laid-back look gets kicked to the curb pretty quickly. "It's a very sharp switch when she enters the Institute and Isabelle gives her those first pieces of clothing," says Phillips. "Those represent the change right there." Enter tighter pants, a tank

The opening scene with Clary outfitted in a custom-dyed green sweater

top, a reworked Nicole Miller dress with zipper details, some cutoff gloves, and high boots.

Phillips admits that of all her work on *City of Bones*, Jace Wayland's principle outfit—which, in fact, was a collaboration of sorts

with Bower—emerges as her favorite, thanks in part to the costume's hood. "We had a conversation on the phone before I met him, and he [said], 'I'd really like to wear a hood.' And I said, 'That sounds like a great idea.' So we built a prototype of a jacket, and we put the hood on it when he came in, and everybody just loved it." (Phillips concedes that the dramatic detail does have its drawbacks. "It's a love-hate relationship," she says, citing the hood's behavior in many of the action sequences. "It does move around a lot. . . . The hood's like another person almost.") But it's worth it for the dramatic effect, such as when Jace and Clary meet for the first time in the

Jace often wears his hood up.

alley behind Java Jones. "The hood just frames [his face], and it looks so amazing," she says. "I thought, 'Wow.' It was a really great moment."

While costumes certainly do a lot to help an actor assume an alter ego, such as a Shadowhunter, vampire, werewolf, and more, clothes alone can't do it all. Makeup often fully realizes a transformation, whether it's through more subtle means such as aging effects or the use of the right smoky eye shadow, or dramatic changes like creating a full face of werewolf hair or the tentacles of a ferocious ravener.

Both director Zwart and head of makeup department Jo-Ann MacNeil knew the impor-

tance of getting the Shadowhunters' rune markings right. "We wanted each character to be unique and distinct but be true to the script," MacNeil says. "Each set of runes was designed with the characters' traits, story, and history in mind. The placement and choices were deliberate to help drive the characters. No two actors had the same rune combinations—even the coloring and size for each actor was tweaked."

MacNeil created concept drawings of the different runes and then worked with the costume department to determine the size and placement of the markings on each performer. The selected designs were then made

City of Bones: The Official Illustrated Movie Companion

into sheets of temporary tattoos for each character, with the individual runes cut out by hand prior to application. Each Shadowhunter wore between ten and twenty different tattoos, each of which was applied to the same spot on an actor's body every day they worked. This process took approximately two hours. "We had to keep track of ordering, replacing, and the application of the tattoos on a daily basis," says MacNeil. Making sure the runes held up during the action scenes presented yet another challenge. "We designed the runes to be as durable as possible, but it was a full-time job to keep them looking sharp during the fight sequences." The makeup team employed a pre-tinted acrylic paint to do touch-ups on set.

EACH SHADOWHUNTER WORE BETWEEN TEN AND TWENTY DIFFERENT TATTOOS, EACH OF WHICH WAS APPLIED TO THE SAME SPOT ON AN ACTOR'S BODY EVERY DAY THEY WORKED.

Makeup artist Jo-Ann MacNeil applies runes to Zegers, while hair stylist Karola Dirnberger touches up his hair.

The Costumes and Makeup of *City of Bones*

The makeup department's work also often reflected a character's emotional and psychological journey over the course of the film. "Hodge was kept captive in the Institute for eighteen years, and we had to show that in his look," says MacNeil. "We faded out his skin tones and dulled down his runes."

Hodge Starkweather prior to his banishment

(Conversely, for a flashback sequence featuring a younger Hodge, the makeup team darkened his rune markings and warmed up his skin tones.) Clary, on the other hand, goes from fresh-faced college girl to novice Shadowhunter. MacNeil showed this evolution by using minimal makeup on Collins at the beginning of the movie and then shifting to a more dramatic look later on. "[Then] her makeup choices had to be strong and powerful but beautiful as well. So for her Shadowhunter look we picked a very smoky brown and copper palette and lightened her skin tone so the colors would pop through." (Clary's fellow female Shadowhunter Isabelle's makeup was always a palette of dark gray and graphite, to match her fierce metal and leather wardrobe.)

And of course, MacNeil and her crew got to break out every color in the makeup kit for the irrepressible Brooklyn warlock Magnus Bane, played by Godfrey Gao. "We decided to try to stay as true to the books as possible," she says. "We built upon the description of his glittery flamboyant personality and used lots of iridescent shiny lipsticks, and a rainbow palette of colors for his nails, eyes, and face."

Some transformations, however, can't be achieved with expert shading, color choices, and application alone, and that's when prosthetics get involved. "Werewolves,

City of Bones: The Official Illustrated Movie Companion

Gao poses as warlock Magnus Bane.

demons, vampires. Creatures of the night. It's a little bit of everything," says special makeup effects designer Paul Jones of his work on *City of Bones*.

The process of creating the movie's gallery of ghouls required some fine-tuning of the vision the director, Zwart, and Jones had at the beginning of shooting. "We did a lot of initial concept designs for creatures and demons that were more leaning toward the creature side of things rather than keeping the more humanoid form," says Jones. "As the movie evolved . . . we realized that a lot of the creatures we created were too much. They were just too elaborate for the style of the movie we were going for, so everything was kind of pared down. We ended up making really ugly people rather than demons because it felt cleaner for the movie. . . . An incredible world has been created by Cassandra Clare, and we didn't want to build too much upon that in terms of grossness. We wanted to keep it streamlined." (Two over-the-top demons did make it on film: the pair of cops Clary encounters leaving Galloway Books. "Everybody loved them, but the style of them didn't fit the movie," says Jones. The duo ended up being toned down digitally in post-production.)

The vampires presented the opposite problem. "We shot a few scenes and realized they weren't enough, so we had to pump them up. We ended up distressing their skin more, making them look more decayed," says Jones. He actually created two kinds of vampires for the movie: the more beautiful crop of bloodsuckers encountered at club Pandemonium—dubbed "glampires" by the crew—and those found back at Hotel Dumort. "[The glampires] look very pretty," says Jones, who used subtle teeth, contact lenses, and pale but not extreme coloring

HE ACTUALLY CREATED TWO KINDS OF VAMPIRES FOR THE MOVIE: THE MORE BEAUTIFUL CROP OF BLOODSUCKERS ENCOUNTERED AT CLUB PANDEMONIUM—DUBBED "GLAMPIRES" BY THE CREW—AND THOSE FOUND BACK AT HOTEL DUMORT.

on the actors in the club scene. "When we get to the Hotel Dumort, which was their home base, their lair, we ended up making them more gross. They're in their own natural habitat; they're not trying to go out in public. It's almost like they revert to their

City of Bones: The Official Illustrated Movie Companion

Two "glampires" attend
Magnus Bane's lucious loft party.

Simon and Isabelle confront glampires at Magnus's party.

natural state, which is slightly decomposing skin tones, black veins. . . . We ended up going more bloodshot with some of the contact lenses; we made larger size dentures. Big, long fingernails."

Lots and lots of fingernails. In addition to making an estimated fifty pairs of dentures for the vampire leads (enlisting the same equipment used by dental technicians), Jones's team created dozens of talonlike fingers for the vampires by modifying oversize cosmetic acrylic nails and augmenting

them to produce thicker claws. For the fight scenes, the same nails were cast in translucent rubber and glued onto the actors' hands. "It means that at the end of the stunt scene we wouldn't have an injury and we'd still have a lot more nails on the actors' fingers," says Jones. "That's the problem when you're doing fingernails. You tend to lose them, so you go through a lot in a day. . . . The last thing I want to do is to be gluing nails on thirty guys after every single take."

For the werewolves, which will ultimately

be rendered as completely CG creatures, Jones's work would help provide the key stage between the characters' transformation from humans to four-legged magical beasts. "It's nice to have a transition stage for a couple of scenes before they go straight into full-grown wolves, because it tells the story better. It helps the audience connect with some of the wolf characters," says Jones. The special makeup effects designer created the transi-tional phase look with full sets of dentures, mutton-chop facial hair pieces, golden contact lenses with enlarged pupils and irises, and prosthetic, clawed fingertips.

Madame Dorothea (or, more accurately, the ravener she would become) was another case of wild sketches at the beginning of filming. "We'd done full-on demon with a mouth the size of her head; big, long tentacle arms; a big, gross neck; and skin fissures splitting and stuff

The primitive vampires of the Hotel Dumort

crawling out of it," says Jones. "It was just too much . . . she's such a fine actress, we realized she could do so much with her performance that we didn't have to go totally gross with the makeup." Jones ended up creating Dorothea's ravener look with Linda Blair's performance

[The Ravener's] trying not to burst out," explains Jones. "We had all these appendages grow out of her body and erupt, so she could do the physicality of the scene without losing the human face because it was a great performance and we didn't want to lose that."

Madame Dorothea slowly turns into a demon with the help of prosthetics.

as the possessed Regan MacNeil in the horror film *The Exorcist* in mind. (Zwart identified the classic genre film as a *City of Bones* inspiration early on to Jones.) "We gave her very similar eyebrows; we gave her very similar facial splits and tears in her skin [to make it look] like there was something underneath. . . .

When asked to identify the toughest work, the most enjoyable work, and the work on the movie of which he's most proud, Jones points to the same job for all three: creating the look for Brother Jeremiah. "He's such an iconic character in the books. He is the one I was most concerned about getting right.

Because the fans have known him for years. They have an image in their head of who he needs to be and what he has to portray in the movie. . . . We didn't want to make him look gross, because he is a good guy. But we also wanted to make him interesting. Something

Brother Jeremiah is bald. Jones ended up crafting an elaborate headpiece that covered the actor's forehead, cheeks, and entire neck, and created a new chin and lips for the character as well. (Jeremiah's eyes will be removed digitally by special effects house Mr. X Inc., in

Brother Jeremiah (played by Stephen Hart) is created by Paul Jones.

kind of grotesque, but you don't want to look away at the same time."

The job would prove not only aesthetically challenging but technically difficult as well, in no small part because the actor playing him, Stephen Hart, sports a full head of long, black hair, and as *City of Bones* fans well know,

accordance with the book's description of the character.) "The only part of [Stephen's] face that remained was his nose tip and his ears. Everything else was prosthetics," confirms Jones. He adds with a note of satisfaction, "People will see that and not realize they're not looking at a bald guy."

FIVE

THE FILMING OF
CITY OF BONES

FROM THE BEGINNING, *CITY OF BONES* DIRECTOR HARALD ZWART KNEW ONE THING FOR SURE: DESPITE THE FACT THAT VIRTUALLY EVERY KIND OF OTHERWORLDLY CREATURE (NOT TO MENTION SOME COMPLETELY NEW ONES) MADE AN APPEARANCE OVER THE COURSE OF THE MOVIE, HE ABSOLUTELY WAS NOT MAKING A HORROR FILM.

As an artist, Clary is frequently sketching people she meets.

"To me this was all about a girl who finds her own strength and discovers what the real truth is, and that there's more out there than meets the eye. All those things that play as a great metaphor for life in general," he says. "I was really intrigued by the intricacy and the complexity and the psychology of all that. . . . What does that do to somebody? You come home, and your mom is gone, and you wake up in the morning, and you've drawn hundreds of weird symbols, and you don't even know that you've drawn them.

What does that do to you as a person? What I thought was really interesting with Clary was that she didn't fold under this pressure. She just goes deeper and deeper. . . . It's like an investigation, a detective story, where she goes into her own history and into her own mind."

Already cast as the movie's heroine Clary Fray when Zwart signed on to direct, actress Lily Collins found Zwart's take on the story both fresh and intriguing. "I remember my first meeting with him on this project, and I was

Clary and Jace learn an awful truth about their history.

listening to him talk about emotion and characters. I kept thinking, 'He can't be talking about the same script.' Because, of course, it had character and emotion, but it was so CGI-based and so imagery-based," she recalls. "And he said, 'I like that, but that's not what this movie's about. It's about characters and people and this girl's story and emotion. And if that's not there, then you're going to lose out on an entire audience. It's great if fans of the book want to see the movie and like the movie, but you want to invite new people in. You don't want to alienate anyone.'"

Zwart wasn't anti-demon, anti-vampire, or anti-Downworlder; he just didn't want the movie's supernatural elements to overshadow, so to speak, the emotional truth at the core of the story. "To me, the monsters and creatures are metaphors and extras," he says. "I use them only to trigger certain things with the character. Because it's a love story between two people who should never fall in love."

When assembling the team to work on the movie, Zwart made sure people checked their horror-movie preconceptions at the door by invoking as a primary influence a much different kind of film: the Academy Award–winning period drama *Amadeus*. "It was a way to get everybody like my director of photography, the production designer, the wardrobe designer, the composer—everybody—to totally reset their mind and look at the movie in a different way," he says. "Because if you come to [the film's composer] Atli Örvarsson and say, 'Hey, we're going to do a teen movie with vampires and werewolves,' his mind goes automatically to one place. Whereas if I say, 'Think of this as *Amadeus* first. It has drama; it has Shakespearean depth; it's people versus people; it's got lies and intrigue; and it all happens inside a flamboyant romantic world,' then his mind goes somewhere else. . . . I just wanted to start off this movie with all the key people at the far opposite end of a normal horror movie, and I knew that we'd end up being somewhere in the healthy middle."

Beyond exalting narrative and character over the movie's Shadow World elements, Zwart also brought an unwavering commitment to realism to both the story and the production. "Harald Zwart has an interesting relationship with magic because he doesn't believe in magic," says producer Robert Kulzer. "So we have a guy who is basically directing a movie that is filled with magic, and he says, 'I'm sorry, but I don't believe in magic. But I want to sort of make it work for my mind.'"

Responds Zwart, "I do believe in magic—and I absolutely believe in movie magic. I love to dream away and believe there are aliens and that people can fly." It turns out that Zwart's original comment to Kulzer was rooted in his desire to start on the opposite end of the spectrum, as he

133   CONTINUED: 133

Clary is jolted back by this confirmation. She can barely
breathe. Then she sees Jace's despair.

                    CLARY
          Valentine's lying. You're Michael
          Wayland's son. Luke told me my
          brother is dead. They found his
          remains in the ashes.

                    VALENTINE
          (I took Jonathan with me when I
          ran.) Those were the bones of a
          child killed by wolves.

                    JACE (*k thyen*)
          I wish it weren't true.

Valentine stares at Clary ~~with amusement~~.

                    VALENTINE
          She doesn't want to believe it
          because she's in love with you,
          ~~Jonathan.~~ *Jonathan*

                    CLARY
          I thought your name was Jace.

                    JACE
          Jace is a nickname.

A precipice opens before Clary.

                    CLARY
          Jonathan Christopher... J.C. Jace.
          Oh, my God.

He seizes her vulnerability.

                    VALENTINE
          Our family, together again. With
          the Cup. (The world is ours to —
          take.) There's no time to waste.

Clary shakes her head, (she won't fall for this.) He grabs
her by the neck and drags her to the table where the
Tarot card is.

                    VALENTINE (CONT'D)
          Take it out.

He pushes her face inches from it. She tries to resist
him. He pushes further, losing his temper.

                    VALENTINE (CONT'D)
          TAKE IT OUT!

                                              (CONTINUED)

Director Zwart's notes on a script page

SIMON
So wait, your mom is gone and
you're hanging out with some dyed-
blond wannabe ~~Goth who just~~ *Girl*
~~trashed your apartment?~~...

She searches through the mess.

CLARY
~~It wasn't him.~~ *He found me*   *
Jace ~~She~~ finds the phone *and hands it to her*

~~Here it is.~~ CLARY (CONT'D)

It's got blood on it. Her heart sinks. With a deep
breath, she quickly goes through the call log.

CLARY (CONT'D)
Clary, Clary, Clary... Simon. She
called you?

She looks at him.

CLARY (CONT'D)
Why didn't you pick up?

SIMON
I-I.. was looking for you. If I'd
known it was serious I would've
picked up.

CLARY
How would you know if you didn't
pick up?   *and she looks over at Jace*

He has no answer. Jace walks back in to show Clary the
vial.

JACE
I found this in her room.
(to Simon)
For the record, my hair is
naturally blond.

Clary shakes her head.

CLARY
What is it?

JACE
Nothing good.

CLARY
We've gotta find Luke.

Remember ; CU- bottle pan up to Jace

(CONTINUED)

Zwart and producer Robert Kulzer on the set of the Institute.

explains further: "The Mortal Instruments world is a fantastic world, but in order to convert it to film, I had to get my head around it a little more. I did not want to cheat, and therefore I needed to at least try to explain most occurrences with physical laws that could be understood.

"For instance, we could use frequencies and vibrations to locate demons or to be able to see through things. A stele, for example, can set an element to vibrate, like a tuning fork, so it suddenly becomes translucent; music and its overtones can have certain effects on certain creatures, like dogs reacting to tones humans can't hear, and so forth.

"Those things fascinated me and I wanted to apply this kind of thinking to The Mortal Instruments. But of course, movie magic inevitably takes over, because not everything can be explained. But at least you have a ground to stand on."

"Harald always says, 'If it's too fantastic, if it's too far out there, I'm not going to believe it. And if I'm not going to believe it, then I

don't believe the audience is going to believe it,'" says producer Don Carmody. "So he [went] for very realistic locations, costumes, casting choices. He wants to believe in the people that are actually there and the spaces that they are in. So they're a little fantastic, but they actually exist. If it gets too fairy tale with all green screen and everything else, he says we're not going to believe it. We have to believe that this place exists within the city."

The director's commitment to making the universe of the film as believable as possible extended to the often intense action scenes. "The actor training was extensive," says Carmody. "Not only was there physical training to get bodies in shape to be able to deal with the stunt training, but then very extensive stunt training. Harald especially wanted to be able to use the actors in as many sequences and as far into the sequence as possible. It's not like, 'Oh no!' and then a stunt guy steps in. I mean, [the actors] know the moves. In the Hotel Dumort both Kevin [Zegers] and Jamie [Campbell Bower] are doing their own flips and spins and all kinds of crazy things. I [was] constantly [thinking], 'Please don't hurt yourself.'"

"There are certain things that you should never let your actor do. You need to have a professional stunt person do it," admits Zwart. "But for anything that's just a little

Using his stele,
Jace carves a rune
into his skin.

challenging, I always had the goal to make sure that they were doing it themselves. . . . I think there's some subliminal satisfaction for the audience [when they do]. And it engages the actors into feeling the fear and the excitement a lot more, if they're in the midst of it themselves. It also helps their performance, obviously."

Stunt coordinator Jean Frenette worked with the actors to prepare them for the demanding sequences and developed individual styles of fighting for each character. For Jonathan Rhys Meyers, who plays the film's villain, Valentine Morgenstern, that meant training in samurai sword work and nineteenth-century épée, as well as the Indonesian martial art *pencak silat* and *wing chun* kung fu for his hand-to-hand combat scenes. "Within the action sequences, everything is almost elegant up until the last moment where it's danger. I think that's what we're trying to achieve as much as possible," says Meyers. "Fighting for films is not like fighting on the street. Fighting on the street is quick; it's nasty; it's sharp. Fighting on film is an elegant dance."

The Shadowhunters kill a demon inside a crowded club and no one but Clary notices.

City of Bones: The Official Illustrated Movie Companion

Bower's intense regimen included a combination of Israeli self-defense technique *krav maga*, sword fighting, knife fighting, hand-to-hand combat, and stunt training.

"Every day he's off, we train together," said Frenette during filming. "We're working on his acrobatic[s]—how to take falls, how to take hits—because he's doing most of it. And then there's the whole fitness training and nutrition. It's very demanding for an actor, because he's got so much to do as well as playing the part. . . . I think it's a luxury for a director to have his actor to be able to do such things."

To Bower, the rigorous workouts not only prepped him for his fight scenes, they gave him the endurance to maintain the film's demanding shooting schedule. "You have to be strong in order to do the stunts, in order to have the stamina to be able to shoot seventeen-hour days and slide across the hood of a car at four o'clock in the morning," said the actor. "You have to be able to pull that out of somewhere, because otherwise you're going to hurt yourself."

"It's funny, every day we get called in to set for hours, but we all still go to the gym every day and train," says Collins. "I don't think anyone understands how exhausting it is to do, to keep it up. But it really pays off when you do an action sequence and it's proven that it's you."

When choreographing the Shadowhunter fight scenes, Frenette worked hard to create a vocabulary of movement unique to the demon killers, with the individual characters possessing their own take on that style. "He [came] up with his own interpretation of Shadowhunter fighting," says Kulzer. "[It's] extremely fluid. . . . He didn't want to do the sort of eastern-influenced fighting. It's very modern, very contemporary, and it has this kind of frenetic attitude. It's short bursts of action."

Actor Kevin Zegers felt that the style of fighting created for his character, Alec Lightwood, made sense for the intense, repressed Shadowhunter. "It says a lot about your character. Especially when you're fighting side by side with people, it makes a difference when the audience knows which

> "YOU HAVE TO BE STRONG IN ORDER TO DO THE STUNTS, IN ORDER TO HAVE THE STAMINA TO BE ABLE TO SHOOT SEVENTEEN-HOUR DAYS AND SLIDE ACROSS THE HOOD OF A CAR AT FOUR O'CLOCK IN THE MORNING."
> —BOWER

Jamie Campbell Bower performs some of his own stunts, as seen here during the vampire fight scene at the Hotel Dumort.

Jace slides across a police cruiser as he prepares to fight demon cops.

one of you it is," the actor says. "I wanted to be able to create a fighting style that represented who he is: very understated but really violent and kind of ferocious. He's an over-killer."

Seeming perfectly at ease with his character's weapon of choice was also crucial to the actor. "For a couple weeks I always had the dagger in my hand, because if you ever see somebody who has a weapon, they're very comfortable

with that weapon," he says. "I wanted Alec to look like he had done this a million times. Because certainly at the beginning of the film, these situations they're finding themselves in are not abnormal, so they need to look like this is just another day at the office."

Any movie filled with assorted supernatural creatures and monumental fight scenes is going to feature some enhancement of reality. In the case of *City of Bones*, the film's ghouls, violent altercations, and more were the result of a collaboration between the visual effects and special effects department.

"I'm a firm believer in getting elements in camera if we can," says the production's visual effects supervisor James Cooper. "If we have it through the lens, that is always the best way to capture things." A prime example of this kind of partnership is the showdown at the Hotel Dumort, which features werewolves crashing through large windows when they come to the aid of the Shadowhunters. "We were shooting what amounted to green duf-

fel bags from air cannons through these large plate glass windows to smash them out," says Cooper. (The visual effects team then takes that footage and superimposes CG werewolves over the images of the duffel bags.)

"We could have done it as a full CG glass-breaking situation . . . but basically, it's a lot more expensive to create a CG breaking-glass element than it is to actually fire a green duffel bag through a window. So that's one consideration for sure," says Cooper. "But [breaking glass] does have a certain chaotic unpredictability that obviously in the visual effects land we try to match as much as possible. But if we can capture it for real, then I think it's always the best way to go."

The Portal would provide another opportunity to meld practical and computer-generated effects. "[A Portal] is something that we've all kind of seen in one form or another in a lot of different movies: this gateway to another dimension sort of thing. We all agreed we wanted ours to have a little bit of a different vibe than we had seen before." The solution would be the use of a large mirrorlike surface made from a material called Mylar that is reflective but also allows light to shine through. "So we have a light coming through, we have a light bouncing off, we have our reflections [of the actors] in there, and all of that lends to a pretty amazing-looking

Kevin Zegers performs some of his own stunts. Here, he is fighting a vampire.

Valentine stares into the reflective, watery surface of the Portal.

in-camera Portal. Then we're going to take that and use CG elements to enhance that," explains Cooper. "It's a really good example of how using partial practical and partial CG elements can wind up creating a much greater whole."

"A lot of the movie is us giving [the visual effects department] elements to run with. So we start it off, and they finish it," says special effects coordinator Tony Kenny. "It always makes it more believable when you start off practical, and then it works into a

visual thing. . . . The fun of it is seeing the end product more than anything."

While *City of Bones* features plenty of excitement and rigorous action sequences, the film's intense psychological drama and high emotional stakes require a cast with formidable acting skill as well—especially for the portrayal of the story's complicated villain, Valentine Morgenstern.

"I get to play a character who brings a very, very dangerous element to a film that is already dangerous," says Meyers. "For the

they create, and we could totally feel [that] with Jonathan."

Collins felt that working with an actor of Meyers's caliber only made her better. "Jonathan Rhys Meyers as Valentine is so fascinating and so intense. When we're shooting, he constantly surprises you with what he brings to the table," she says. "He is so intense and so brilliant. . . . When a really amazing actor works opposite you, it just ups your game. . . . He makes you really feel what the scene's about."

In Collins, Zwart found a lead actress capable of exhibiting the range of emotions

last twenty minutes, once Valentine enters, it heightens everyone's fear of what's going to happen and what's going to happen in the future. This is almost like chapter one."

Producer Kulzer says that Meyers's work on the film had quite an impact on set. "There's something of a wild animal in the performance that he does as Valentine," he says. "And we could feel it. He brought this new energy to the cast. Jamie walked up to me and said, 'I'm a bit scared of him.' And Lily walked up to me and said, 'He's great, but I'm a bit scared of him.' And I said, 'Yeah, that's what it's supposed to be like.' Great actors, there's a certain energy field that

Valentine dangerously clutches Clary close.

experienced by Clary. "I loved working on the subtleties with Lily. . . . [This] could quickly have become one of those movies where the main character walks through the whole movie with one expression. Because [Clary] is constantly thrown new challenges, she could just walk around with a deer-caught-in-the-headlights look all through the movie," the director says. "I wanted to make her strong; I wanted to make her funny; I wanted to make her surprised, scared—all those things. And there was no stock acting. It was always digging deeper. We had long conversations about where [Lily] could relate it to her own life. . . . Nothing we did felt false."

Zwart and Collins fine-tune the opening balcony scene.

"I WANTED TO MAKE HER STRONG; I WANTED TO MAKE HER FUNNY; I WANTED TO MAKE HER SURPRISED, SCARED—ALL THOSE THINGS. AND THERE WAS NO STOCK ACTING. IT WAS ALWAYS DIGGING DEEPER. WE HAD LONG CONVERSATIONS ABOUT WHERE [LILY] COULD RELATE IT TO HER OWN LIFE. . . . NOTHING WE DID FELT FALSE."
—DIRECTOR HARALD ZWART

"What I thought was really interesting about working with Lily on her performance was [that] it was like you could almost fine-tune, like you fine-tune on the radio," says Zwart. "[I would] just say little things to her, and the performance changed."

Zwart took a collaborative approach when directing the actors, trusting the performers' instincts on everything from the phrasing of a certain line to movement in a scene. "I approached it a little bit as you would direct a stage play. . . . It was very rare that I dictated them to be in a certain space, because I needed them there for the sake of the camera. So I did a lot of rehearsing with them where we walked the scenes and we moved things around, and if it felt awkward for them to be close, then we separated them. So the blocking in the movie was very much dictated by the intentions of the actors and the characters. . . . And that's because they started to really take possession of the characters, so they could really follow them emotionally."

"The process of working with Harald is very organic . . . it is very much about feeling out a scene," says Bower. "If we go into a scene and we say, 'I'm not entirely sure I would say that,' or 'At this point it feels a bit sticky. Can we do something to change it?' Harald is very happy to be able to move things around and

is accommodating of his actors while also having his own vision of what he wants."

Collins found the director's enthusiasm infectious. "He's so energetic. He's always like, 'I am so unbelievably ready! Who's ready? Let's go!' That's what you need. Especially when we're doing long hours in dark environments—they're stuffy and you're tired. You need someone to helm that ship who is passionate, who loves the story, has great ideas, and is open to hearing yours."

The man who would bring the vision of the greenhouse—and the rest of Cassandra Clare's evocative settings—to the big screen was production designer François Séguin. A French Canadian whose work ranges from designs for live productions, such as operas and Cirque du Soleil shows, to Showtime's period drama *The Borgias* and Zwart's previous movie *The Karate Kid*, Séguin created a luxurious, richly detailed world for the movie's characters to inhabit. "François Séguin is a brilliant production designer," says producer Carmody. "He's really stepped up on this one, and this is not his usual type of movie, but he's just gone with it and created some astonishing sets and set pieces. The greenhouse was one of the most romantic sets I've ever been in."

"François's vision is a very heavily detailed vision," says *City of Bones* art director

Anthony Ianni. "When we're building a set, he continues to add detail right up until the last minute, and it's beautiful. There's certainly a visual interest that's beyond anything I've seen before."

In order to capture that richness, Zwart made what is an increasingly rare choice: to shoot on film. "Five years ago every single movie was shot on film, and now digital seems to be the only way to go," he says. "What film was able to do was to preserve the softness of the skin tones and the romance. If I had done a science fiction movie or a more hard-core street movie or the straightforward action movie, I would have considered something else. But to me this was always about the powdery feel to the skin tones, the romance, the blurry backgrounds, the textures—all that

Production designer François Séguin touches up the set.

City of Bones: The Official Illustrated Movie Companion

The set of the greenhouse

stuff that film captures naturally. . . . So to me it was just a very natural step, and thankfully, the producers supported that."

New York City is a fantastic locale to use as the setting of an urban fantasy epic, as The Mortal Instruments series and *City of Bones* clearly illustrates. Due to logistics and cost, however, it's not the easiest place to shoot a movie. Which is why Zwart and crew set up shop in Toronto, Canada, to film *City of Bones*. Locations ranged from a club on the west side of Toronto (Pandemonium) and an abandoned hotel (Hotel Dumort), to an early twentieth-century conservatory (the greenhouse) and a Hamilton, Ontario, graveyard (the City of Bones's exterior). Certain sets, like the Institute, were shot in several locations. "We had to stitch the Institute together," says Zwart. "We had the corridors in one location. Steps were in another location. Entrance in yet another location. So it was a little bit of patchwork to put it together." Still more sets, such as the Brooklyn brownstone, the library, and the dome, were crafted by a team of carpenters. "We did go all over the place," concedes Zwart.

Zwart on set with the director of photography, Geir Hartly Andreassen.

City of Bones: The Official Illustrated Movie Companion

The Fray brownstone

Simon walks down a "Brooklyn" street.

City of Bones: The Official Illustrated Movie Companion

"The director of photography, Geir Hartly Andreassen, and I just ran between a couple of cameras during the day. . . . You set up one shot, and then you run over to the other one."

As far as making Toronto look like New York, according to Zwart, it's not as hard as one would think. "They do look similar. . . . The street feels the same; the downtown area feels the same. So it's almost as simple as adding yellow cabs, New York City policemen, some mailboxes, and you're there," says the director, who also traveled to New York to shoot a few aerial and establishing shots of photo doubles crossing the street to cement the illusion. "Once you put that together, the audience has no reason to doubt that they're in New York City."

For Zwart, replicating New York City is easy; doing justice to the rich and textured world of The Mortal Instruments, however, is another matter. The director is realistic about what he's up against. "I don't think anything can overcome what your imagination or your mind's eye can give you," he says, thinking of the series' millions of readers. "But the film will for sure open it up to an audience who hasn't read the books, and hopefully, the fans will be happy with what they see."

Zwart did make sure to include at least one thing he knows every fan will love: an

> "I DON'T THINK ANYTHING CAN OVERCOME WHAT YOUR IMAGINATION OR YOUR MIND'S EYE CAN GIVE YOU. BUT THE FILM WILL FOR SURE OPEN IT UP TO AN AUDIENCE WHO HASN'T READ THE BOOKS, AND HOPEFULLY, THE FANS WILL BE HAPPY WITH WHAT THEY SEE."
> —DIRECTOR HARALD ZWART

appearance by the person who conjured the all-encompassing world of The Mortal Instruments in the first place. "I really wanted to put Cassandra in there, so she has a little cameo at Magnus Bane's," he reveals. "That's a party scene where there's a lot of creatures. So I said, 'That's where you should be. You should be amongst all these things that you've created yourself.'"

Look out for author Cassandra Clare's cameo during Magnus Bane's party scene.

SIX

THE FANS OF
CITY OF BONES

THROUGH 2012, OVER TWO MILLION COPIES OF *THE MORTAL INSTRUMENTS: CITY OF BONES* HAVE BEEN SOLD. THAT'S NOT JUST A LOT OF BOOKS; THAT'S A LOT OF FANS. AND CASSANDRA CLARE'S FANS ARE A DEEPLY DEVOTED, PASSIONATE BUNCH—WHO NO DOUBT WOULD BE HAPPY TO GO HEAD TO HEAD WITH POTTER-HEADS AND TWIHARDS ANY DAY OF THE WEEK.

As an author, Clare has a special bond with her readers. Long before Hollywood came calling, the writer cultivated a relationship with her audience through her website, book signings, social media, and more. "Cassandra has a very, very strong hold on her fans. They trust her. And she trusts them," says producer Robert Kulzer. "She is almost like the mother figure of her fans."

Not long after the release of *City of Bones*, sites paying tribute to the world of The Mortal Instruments, through original art and fan fiction, started popping up all over the Web. Clare embraces her readers' interpretations of the characters she's crafted. "I think fan art is wonderful," she told racebending.com. "I have very creative and talented fans and feel blessed."

It goes without saying that when word of a *City of Bones* movie surfaced, Clare's fans rejoiced. And they followed the entire process of making the film—from initial casting rumors to shooting to the premiere—with unbridled excitement.

Clare's fans' enthusiasm surprised even veteran producer Don Carmody. "These aren't your usual fanboys. . . . These are very bright young adults who read and love these books for what they are," he said on set in Toronto. "We have these hoards of teenage

> "THESE ARE VERY BRIGHT YOUNG ADULTS WHO READ AND LOVE THESE BOOKS FOR WHAT THEY ARE."
> —PRODUCER DON CARMODY

"The Mortal Instruments
series is a story world
that I love to live in.
Beautiful!"
—STEPHENIE MEYER
AUTHOR OF *Twilight*

#1 *New York Times* Bestselling Series

THE MORTAL INSTRUMENTS
Book One

City of Bones
CASSANDRA CLARE

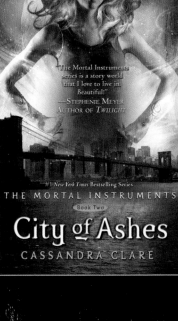

The Mortal Instruments
series is a story world
that I love to live in.
Beautiful!"
—STEPHENIE MEYER
AUTHOR OF *Twilight*

#1 *New York Times* Bestselling Series

THE MORTAL INSTRUMENTS
Book Two

City of Ashes
CASSANDRA CLARE

"The Mortal Instruments
series is a story world
that I love to live in.
Beautiful!"
—STEPHENIE MEYER
AUTHOR OF *Twilight*

#1 *New York Times* Bestselling Series

THE MORTAL INSTRUMENTS
Book Three

City of Glass
CASSANDRA CLARE

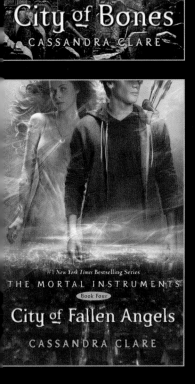

#1 *New York Times* Bestselling Series

THE MORTAL INSTRUMENTS
Book Four

City of Fallen Angels
CASSANDRA CLARE

#1 *New York Times* Bestselling Series

THE MORTAL INSTRUMENTS
Book Five

City of Lost Souls
CASSANDRA CLARE

#1 *New York Times* Bestselling Prequel to the Mortal Instruments Series

THE INFERNAL DEVICES
· Book One ·

Clockwork Angel
CASSANDRA CLARE

#1 *NEW YORK TIMES* BESTSELLER

THE INFERNAL DEVICES
· Book Two ·

Clockwork Prince
CASSANDRA CLARE

THE INFERNAL DEVICES
· Book Three ·

The sequel to the #1 *New York Times* bestseller CLOCKWORK PRINCE

Clockwork Princess
CASSANDRA CLARE

Cassandra Clare and her husband, Josh, on set with Zwart in Toronto

girls and young guys hanging out. They find out where we shoot every day. Somehow they find out. And they're there. They're all clutching the book—and they aren't pushy; they don't bother us. They just want to be part of the experience. I've never experienced anything like that."

Director Harald Zwart was similarly impressed with the fans' dedication. "We had groups of fans waiting outside the hotel. We had fans waiting outside our sets when we were on location. They were there every day," he says. "Even when we had night shoots. We'd be shooting all night, and I went home at seven in the morning—they were still there! So they are truly loyal, great fans."

While Clare's readers are clearly grateful to her for creating such a wonderful and fantastic world, the author is thankful for the sense of community her fans have created, and she is elated to share the thrill of seeing the people and places of The Mortal Instruments on the big screen with them. "As an author, one of the most amazing parts of the experience is to be able to create a world that starts off in your head but then so many other people can live in. . . . I think one of the really amazing things about the film being made is that it's going to sort of unite the Shadowhunters from all over the world into being able to all share one experience. . . . I think that it's going to be an amazing experience that I'm going to be able to have with my fans. I'm really looking forward to it," she says. "It really is wonderful not to feel like I'm alone in my excitement, [but instead] to feel like I'm part of this huge group of people who are incredibly excited."